BONE & JUICE

Books by Adrian C. Louis

POETRY

The Indian Cheap Wine Seance (1974)

Muted War Drums (1977)

Sweets for the Dancing Bears (1979)

Fire Water World (1989)

Among the Dog Eaters (1992)

Days of Obsidian, Days of Grace (1994)

Blood Thirsty Savages (1994)

Vortex of Indian Fevers (1995)

Ceremonies of the Damned (1997)

Skull Dance (1998)

Ancient Acid Flashes Back (2000)

Bone & Juice (2001)

FICTION

Skins (1995)

Wild Indians & Other Creatures (1996)

BONE & JUICE

Adrian C. Louis

TRIQUARTERLY BOOKS
NORTHWESTERN UNIVERSITY PRESS
Evanston, Illinois

TriQuarterly Books
Northwestern University Press
Evanston, Illinois 60208-4210

Printed in the United States of America

10 9 8 7 6 5 4 3 2 1

ISBN 0-8101-5115-4 (cloth)
ISBN 0-8101-5116-2 (paper)

Library of Congress Cataloging-in-Publication Data

Louis, Adrian C.
Bone & juice / Adrian C. Louis.
p. cm.
ISBN 0-8101-5115-4 (cloth) — ISBN 0-8101-5116-2 (pbk.)
I. Title.
PS3562.O82 B66 2001
811'.54—dc21
2001003987

For Colleen, forever, more or less.
As it was in the beginning, is now,
and ever shall be, world without end.

J'ensevelis les morts dans mon ventre.
Cris, tambour, danse, danse, danse, danse!
Je ne vois même pas l'heure où, les blancs
débarquant, je tomberai au néant.
—Arthur Rimbaud

Contents

Acknowledgments

Some of these poems first appeared in *Skull Dance*, a chapbook published in 1998 by Bull Thistle Press.

Other poems, some in earlier versions, appeared in *Kenyon Review, Ploughshares, North Dakota Quarterly, New Letters, Salt Hill Journal, Spirit Horse, Nerve Cowboy, Bloomsbury Review, Cortland Review, Cream City Review, Cedar Hill Review, Luna, Missouri Review, Water Stone, Midwest Quarterly, Solo, Main Street Rag, Fire, Café Review, Rattle, Temple, Progressive*, and in the anthologies *Poets of the New Century*, MUAE: *Contagion, Hey Lew*, and *The Best of the Best: A Poetic Chrestomathy*. The author extends gratitude to the editors of these publications and especially to the editors of *Ploughshares*, who selected "This Is the Time of Grasshoppers and All That I See Is Dying" as the recipient of the 2001 Cohen Award.

Special thanks to Reg Gibbons and Sue Betz of Northwestern University who edited this collection of poems. The epigraph referring to Lew Welch is by Elisabeth Sherwin and is reprinted with permission. Finally, I would like to thank Leslie for the transfusions in the midst of my most recent confusions. *Gracías*.

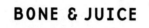

BONE & JUICE

Valentine from Indian Country

On these plains the plows
and drums wrestle for centuries
and marry into resignation.
The old songs scratch the earth
attempting to release the ancestors.
Digging deeper, John Deere tractors
unleash the Ghost Dance
but nobody remembers the steps.

Cattle and deer graze together
in the moonlit fields, both
afraid of civilization, and
fearful of the forgetful
mouth of man.

My crazy friend Bob used to
tell me he thought drinking
was a revolutionary act.
Of course, this was before
he got out of his car
in a Badlands blizzard
and lurched until he turned
into a block of brown ice.

Months after my near-fatal
operation I ask my doctor

if I can drink again.
I didn't know you drank.
Well, I haven't in ten years,
I tell him and shake my head.
I've paid my dues and I'm
still a bloodthirsty fool.
I leave his office and sigh,
knowing I've made it
through another day.
Ten years of one day at a time.
O sweet Mary of Nazareth,
my soul is the Black Rock Desert
and your Son is not my wine.

Crossing into the rez,
most white people think
they're entering hell.
There is an unmistakable scent
of brimstone, eternal damnation.
Everywhere they turn are burned-out
husks of abandoned cars and scarred
husks of abandoned humans,
shuffling, lost in the dreams of
their grandfathers.
Hope is only a word used
in grant applications or in
the leering glare of casino
one-armed bandits.

Yes, this is Indian Country
and we are bone and juice,
twelve frothy ounces of moon
drool, a touch of inexact wistfulness,
wry evaporation, and eventual extinction.
In America there is no truer place
for us to worship our terrible beauty.

Shades of Green

This is how it is.
I have a new motto:
This Nebraska bordertown
is the best that I can do.

The hamburger I got
for dinner was green.
Even my dogs wouldn't eat it.
It's a harsh late-spring night.
Early P.M. rain turns to snow
making the roads sheet ice.
My wife is in the nursing home
with early onset Alzheimer's disease.
I am sleepless with aches and pains,
magnified by middle-aged hypochondria
and money worries. I toss and turn on
my jaded couch, fighting for space
with furball felines and canines.

Slightly past midnight the police
scanner says a young girl is speeding
here from Pine Ridge with no lights
on, driving a green VW Jetta on ice roads.
No lights! What is her problem?
Green girl, must I pray for you too?

This life I've lived is a prayer for you.

Skin & Bones

Bones of dream.
Broken bones.
Bones of creation.
Bones that were.
I have broken you
and the marrow
blood bubbles into
crimson wings.
City of Angels.
Pico & Union, 1982.
Oh, sweet Christ,
there was a Cheyenne
domme and fillet of soul.
Lavender jacaranda
and liquid-fire sky.
Smoke of a dying nation
and swarming gangsters
on the stoops when I
left for the Dakotas.
I pity the fool I was.
I pity the *was* that
fools me now.
Nineteen years
of prairie ennui
and skeletal moves.
Joint against joint.

White-powder footsteps.
Infinity masquerading as
the not-so-great
Great Plains.

Juice

Evaporated juice.
Canned juice.
I turn the can
opener of memory.
She walks into my house
like she owns it.
Making sloppy joes
for the softball tournament.
Twelve years ago, tight, tight shorts.
Tight white shorts, firm butt
cheeks blaring out at me.
Made my move, yes.
Let me Polaroid your legs.
Nice, but I need them shiny.
Baby oil up thighs, higher.
Baby oil on our frantic hearts.

Ghost of juice now.
Her cancer baldness now.
Indian cemetery whispering.
Nothing I can really say.
What should I say?
Do you remember?
Wasn't it good? I mean
wasn't it good and hot and sweet?

You sure were pretty
before you started dying!

Oh, withered, arid plains of August.
No juice now, nor ever again.

Song of Arrows

Ooooooooo. Oooooooooooooooooooo.
That high, lonesome sound you hear?
It's ghosts of blue soldiers marching,
stumbling through moonless night.
A homesick trooper lights a cigarette
trying to recall an old anthem
and the soft melody returns
with the hush and whistle
of hand-hewn arrows.

We sing that song of arrows
in the bordertown stores when
they follow us down the aisles
to make sure we don't steal.

We sing that song of arrows
when Indian-hating cops stop us
for no reason on desolate highways.

We sing that song of arrows while
we tiptoe on the outskirts
of this sad and goofy
movie named *America.*
It's got a good beat.
You can dance to it
if you're drunk enough.

In the Land of the No Hearts

FOR SISTER ANNEMARIE

One of these centuries when
I'm mature and not so sober
I'll write a novel of
autonomous, anonymous
Indian Territory in 1856,
long before I fell in love
with Emmylou Harris
and prescription drugs . . .

I

Masturbating, the full moon
grabs its drab whiteness
back from the drifted snow.
The earth is without color,
only the black of burned
and shattered pines dead
long before the knife
of winter slashed.

From a nearby village,
a wisp of smoke and light

rises sly and wary
of the deviant globe.
A broken woman who
once held the weight
of the world upon her
shoulders is crying.
She's old, but not ancient.
She cannot take care
of herself and the village
is low on food. Her own
relatives resent her now.
All their tears are long dry.
They have come to scorn
her weird words and gait.
The moon, she says to them.
The moon is full.
Once I had a life just like you.
I had a good, full life, but
don't leave me alone.

I am not ready
to leave all I know.

The People are packed
and ready to journey.
Nobody answers her.
Nobody looks at her.
She is dead in the eyes
and ears of her kin.
Now, the entire village
is on the move under
the malevolent moon.

Once I had a life,
she whispers at the backs
of her rapidly vanishing blood.

Where are your hearts,
my People?
Please answer me!
You care more
about dogs than me!

Please answer me!
Where are your hearts?

II

One hard year passed.
For weeks the People
watched the comet.
Beyond its tail,
something trailed.
Some said it was
the spirit of death.
Some said it was
the hand of the Creator
himself, that the comet
was a hot coal he held
to light the way of those
walking upon the ghost road.

One night when the comet
was at its brightest, some say

they heard an old woman
weeping and in the morning
every heart in the village
had vanished. Gone.
The breasts of the People
would never pulse
with love again.

Colleen, today my mind ran
rabid attempting to explain
why some of us cannot
explain our inability
to love except to mumble
those clichés about the boarding
schools and how they changed
most Skins from men to rocks . . .

E-Mail to a High School Sweetheart
Who Recently Tracked Me Down

It's only slightly apocryphal
when I tell you a tale of
northern Nevada, 1889, when
Pah-Nah-Kee stood before
the Black Rock Desert
and thought of the *taibo*
woman who'd encouraged
him to fly to her like a night
hawk in its dark hunger.
Tell me how I can fly
with wings made of lies?
he'd softly answered
at their last meeting.

He could not leave his dark
world for a white skin.
He'd grown up on hot, alkaline
soil pulsing with pale yellow
scorpions and scruffy rabbits
scurrying from the taunts
of his ancestor spirits.

It's only slightly apocryphal
when I tell you that more
than a hundred years later
an invisible line would
appear in the dirt that the

great-grandson of Pah-Nah-Kee
would limp toward but never
cross—or maybe he'd cross it
but nobody would have
the courage or energy
to tell him . . .
that to return
to the home
that never was
is the ultimate
nightmare of half-breeds.

And . . . in the end, deep down
half of me believes white women
will only break red hearts and balls.
I hope this begins to explain why
I won't be flying to Reno.
It's as good a lie as any.

Song of the Snake

Several years slithered by
and then an honor song
played on KILI-FM is how I find
you passed to the spirit world.
First thought: The snake grew back.
There are some of us the snake will not
bite at all; we're either lucky or cursed.
Others will get bit, punch the snake in
the eyeball, and toss it away forever.

And others of us will get bit, yank
the snake away, and leave the teeth
embedded in our inflamed flanks.
We'll be fine for a while, then those
fangs will begin to gestate; eventually
the snake will grow back full sized
and spitting, guiding us to stand
with shit-pants and wild, holy eyes,
hands out, begging for a cure.

Cousin . . . that was you
with the White Clay shakes
when last we met.

Sasquatch Sonata

Poet Lew Welch was last seen on San Juan Ridge in Nevada County, California, on May 23, 1971. On that day, he took his revolver, left behind a despondent note, and disappeared. Friends and neighbors scoured the area on foot and horseback but never found a trace of the 44-year-old Beat Poet.
—Elisabeth Sherwin

Nebraska Panhandle,
just past the millennium,
and good old Public
Radio is covering
the inaugural address
of the new shrub of
a President and I think
back eight years to the
first inauguration
of the Arkansas
cockhound and I
can't help but recall
the rich, black poet
inside my battered
radio who intoned in
an old-time-preacher
voice, so awkwardly
stringing a necklace
of dead tree branches,
chunks of concrete, and

Simply Good Morning!
to a hopeful but brain
dead America and the fat,
newly elected President by
her side was so blissfully
unaware of the comic
weightlessness of her words.

The passing of eight years
has little to show for it.
I've gained a few pounds,
my woman has gone insane,
and two of my dogs have died,
but when I look out the window
I continue to see the blond
children of the New Aryan Army
goose-stepping past my house
in this Indian-hating little town.
Today, when I'm driving ever
so slowly to the nearest Safeway
I see below a ridge of ponderosas
in a fallow cornfield between
Chadron and Bordeaux Creek,
a huge bright billboard with
the face of a sleek black
man, maybe Air Jordan,
I'm not sure, but he's
wearing dark glasses and
a can of Coke is reflected
in his shades and, Oh man,
there's not a single black

family for a hundred miles
in any of the four sacred
directions and that's the way
the white farmers like it
and, God, they'll tell you
it's bad enough dealing
with us Indians and our shit
and damn—there's something
fleeting through the pines,
dark and covered with hair,
moving fast, a speeding blur
and it might be a Sasquatch
or maybe Lew Welch down
from the hills to cop
some Twinkies and talk.

On the Pungent Outskirts
of Cowturdville, Nebraska

The three-by-four
foot sign is green with
a picture of a jumbo jet
and no words at all.
It stands at the junction
of Highway 20 and the dirt
road leading to the airport:
two forlorn tin sheds sheltering
two ancient cropdusters.
Cowturdville International:
the only airport in hell.

Speeding by, I toss my empty
O'Doul's bottle at the sign.
Tonight I turned fifty
and I'm as immature
as I was at eighteen.
I'm alone, but I won't
drink real beer until my
old lady is done doing her
holy dance of dementia
in the nursing home.

I've got a small bag
of oily popcorn
from the Pump
& Pantry and I'm

watching the speeding
movie of night beyond
the layer of dead bugs
on the windshield
of my '85 Crown Vic.
I see a thin slice
of cantaloupe moon.
I hear no cars at all
and feel nothing but
the cold hardness
of a Czech .38 tucked
snugly into my lazy
American groin.

My life has become
as shallow as a wine
splashed Bukowski poem
and for some perverse
reason I have come
to accept and cherish
the ennui of the mundane.

I have dervished love's dirt
roads for fifty long years
and still have a hard-on
I cannot relieve.

Manifest Destination

This bright hell is America.
A hot wind curls the leaves
and chases the dogs to dig
deep into the baked soil.
It's 107° today and grasshoppers
from outer space are dancing
nasty in my boiling brain.
The air conditioner is broke
so I run a tub of cold water
and submerge every half hour.
There's a wet trail from the bath
to the couch and nearby fan.

The air is so heavy with grain
dust it clouds the eyes.
The *wheaties* are up from
forlorn Oklahoma with
their caravan of combines.
I crave winter. I want a blizzard
that blinds me to my fellow man.
Give me Arctic brain fever
or igloo incapacitation.

These are my sunset days.
Every other day I grieve for the me
that was and most every man or
woman I see fills me with contempt.

Seven out of eleven Skins in town
are hang-around-the-fort welfare addicts
with no clue to breaking the cycle.
Every weekend their drunken madness
fills the county jail where they're
happy to suck the public teat, but
I'm far beyond embarrassment
because the whites in town
are even worse actors.

It goes beyond the cliché that most
white people in Cowturdville
could be hillbillies except for
the fact that these are the Plains.
Their Christian souls simply
cannot digest the pain
of Indians.

So, drive on, rednecks, to the edge
of your flat world and fall
down to a better hell
where half-million-dollar
combines are eating
the heart of these prairies
and you have one lucky
foot out of the flaming
lake of poverty.

Here, in this Panhandle town,
farm kids speed desperately up
and down the main drag wearing
their baseball caps backward, hands

out the windows, stackin', throwing
gang signs they've seen on the tube
while their parents, almost glad
they are no longer young, sit home
and smile and pray to God that
the programs on the TV will
stop using so many cusswords . . .

I haven't been laid
in more than four years
but there's this fat lady,
Louise, with varicose veins
who calls me late at night
and begs me to come over
to her trailer for a drink.
I don't drink, I tell her.

I DON'T drink, I remind myself
but it's a daily struggle to stop
myself from reenrolling in
the College of Beer and Barley.
As far as I can tell, I'm the only
one on my street who's gone
to college and I often wish I
never had, but jeez Louise,
I think I'm starting to like
it here in this American
heartland.

Thunderheads are forming
and the sweet-ass rain
of forgiveness is in the air.

Migraine

Alien, armored,
sexual, robotic.
The filthy grasshoppers
this year hatch these
adjectives and more.
Satan's spawn blankets
my sorry yard and sends
shivers up the spine
of my little house
on the prairie.
These bugs burrow
into my arteries
and shoot out
my penis to clot
on my forehead
and form a thorny
crown of irony.

Oh, Cowturdville!
Your blessed, throbbing
evening arrives and drives
a red-hot lance into my brain.
I don't mind. And I don't mind
these grasshoppers pounding
nails through my wrists,

but someone's got to stop
that stupid prairie moon
from drooling upon
this stolen land.

This Is the Time of Grasshoppers
and All That I See Is Dying

Colleen,
this is the time of grasshoppers
and all that I see is dying except
for my virulent love for you.

The *Cowturdville Star-Times,*
which usually has a typo
in every damn column,
says the grasshoppers this year
"are as big as Buicks" and
that's not bad, but then we
get two eight-point pages
of who had dinner with whom
at the bowling alley café and
who went shopping at Target
in Rapid City and thus the high
church of Adrian the Obscure is sacked.

Even my old Dylan tapes are fading,
becoming near-comic antiques.
The grasshoppers are destroying
our yard and they're as big as
my middle finger saluting God.
The grass is yellow. The trees
look like Agent Orange has hit
but it's only the jaw-work of those
drab armored insects who dance
in profusion and pure destruction.

Sweet woman, dear love of my life,
when you're not angry and sputtering
at everything and everyone, you
become so childlike, so pure.
Your voice seems to have grown
higher recently, almost a little-girl pitch.

Today, like most days, I have you
home for your two-hour reprieve
from the nursing home prison.
We're sitting at the picnic table in
the backyard staring at the defoliation
of lilacs, brain matter, and honeysuckle.
You're eating a Hershey Bar and
a crystal glob of snot is hanging
from your nose.
I reach over, pinch it off,
and wipe it on my jeans.
You thrust the last bite
of chocolate into my mouth
as a demented grasshopper
jumps onto your ear.
You scream. I howl
with laughter until you do too.
Happiness comes with a price.

This is the time of grasshoppers
and all that I see is dying except
for my swarming love for you.

Last night on PBS some
lesioned guy being screwed to death

by legions of viral invisibility
blurted the great cliché of regret:
I wish I could be twenty
again and know what
I know now . . .

My own regrets are equally foolish.
And, I wonder, how the hell
is it I've reached a place
where I'd give what's left
of my allotment of sunsets
and frozen dinners
for some unholy replay
of just one hour in some nearly
forgotten time and place?

Darling,
in the baked soil of the far west,
I first saw the ant lions, those
hairy little bugs who dug funnel
traps for ants in the dry earth.
At twelve, looking over the edge
of one such funnel surrounded by
a circle of tiny stones in the sand,
I aimed a beam of white light
from my magnifying glass
and found I could re-create
a hell of my own accord.

Poverty and boredom
made me cruel early on.
The next summer while digging

postholes I found a cache of
those grotesque yellow bugs
we called Children of the Earth
so I piled matches atop them
and barbecued their ugliness.
I was at war with insects.

In my fifteenth summer I got
covered with ticks in the sagebrush
and that fall I nervously lost my cherry
in a cathouse called the Green Front
and got cursed with crabs but that's
not what I want to sing about
at all . . . come on now.
This is no bug progression.
This ain't no insect sonata.

This is only misdirection,
a sleight of hand upon the keys
and the unholy replay of just
one hour in some nearly
forgotten time and place
that I'd like to return to
will remain myth or maybe
a holy, tumescent mystery.

And let's not call
these bloodwords
POETRY or a winter count
of desperate dreams
when reality is much simpler.

Colleen,
I swear to Christ
this is the time of grasshoppers
and all that I see is dying except
for my sparkling love for you.

Leaves of Grass

*Old age is the most unexpected of all things
that happen to a man.*
—Leon Trotsky

A retired farmer in his late sixties bought the corner double
lot across the street and razed a fine old Victorian that need-
ed some hard work. He put up a prefab house in less than a
week, cut down a dozen ancient hackberry and linden trees,
then paved his yard with sod. Now at least three times a
week this goofy, old redneck roars his riding mower over
the grass at six in the morning and shakes me from my
middle-aged nightmares. Holy shit . . . and when he's not
mowing, he's watering the hell out of his lawn with his
sprinkler system. Is this industry or madness? Gorge the
grass and slice its head off. A huge, green beast to be dealt
with. Strange, this forlorn old farmer waiting for the Reaper.
I hope his constant harvesting isn't an indication of the
onset of Alzheimer's. Some weeks he mows three days in a
row; could he have forgotten? On many mornings I think of
running my twelve gauge out the window and helping him
on his way. Other times I simply marvel at his apparent
good physical health. But most days I wonder why I chose
to make enemies with the white man's God. I pray for for-
giveness but hear only distant thunder, muted laughter, and

sharp blades chomping grass. Green blood dripping off metal. Sweet juice of Babylon. O tart, shivering Christ on the cross. Soon we'll come face to trembling face and swoon . . . and kiss . . . and I'll knee-beg to be the mower of heaven.

High Plains Weather Report

FOR CHARLIE MEHRHOFF

I'm getting colder
as I grow older.
This is the first week
of August and the high
today is a shuddering 52°
and I'm rubbing my hands
together to make fire.
My dogs are out in the chill
howling at the noon siren.
If I let it, it would sadden me
that I have never seen a wolf
in the wild and never will.

Man has corrupted and killed
everything, and now the weather
has finally gone mad too.

Somewhere inside the crystal
clear lines of television, we lost
the illusion of kind, blue skies
and those amber waves of grain.
Somewhere in suburban malls
or maybe in the hoods of the inner

cities, we lost our hopeful souls.
And we've exported that loss
around the entire globe.
Huh?
Around the entire globe?

No, no, *uno momento.*
The weather of madness
was exported here centuries ago.
It came with Pope-addled Spaniards
who, lacking *duende,* killed more
Indians than Hitler killed Jews.
Shicklgruber, Spaniards, wolves,
and worry . . . endless,
insidious, spastic worry.
I'm blaming El Niño.

El Niño is making me goofy.
I'm contemplating buying Viagra.
I might change my name
to Bocephus or James Dean
and buy a Harley and kick
the ass of every high school boy
in town who wears his cap backward.
Then I'll go down to the Main Street
bars and line dance with the locals.
Uh, yeah, that'll be me
screaming YEEEEE-HAAAAA.

What I Yelled at Those Little Gray Aliens Who Abducted Me

Why me? I'm no Sacajawea.

I bet you think you're too cool
when you grab me at the dumpster
in the alley behind my house
where I've gone at midnight
to discard shredded poems.

I'm barely computer literate
so it puzzles me that
you'd beam me aboard
your phallic, pulsing craft.

But you don't know shit from
Shinola if you think I'll spill the beans.
You midget-dick twinks, I'll never tell
you about the men who were men
when I was a boy, those who were
stink-scented with exploded meat
from Anzio and Corregidor
and now are all dead or
imprisoned in nursing homes.
*So, go for it, probe my flesh
and drink my blood.*

And I won't rat on my classmates
who humped the jungles

of rotten-crotch Asia and
are now contemplating AARP.
Nor will I betray that shambling
middle-aged man in my mirror
who has my eyes, but is
no one I can claim.
So, go for it, probe my flesh
and drink my blood.

I guess I can tell you
I'm finally old enough to tolerate
the fact that television accommodates,
glorifies the young and the stupid,
and, by all accounts, even the previous
President of these United States refused
to act his age and keep his fly zipped
up and I suppose I envied him except
for the fact that he was from Arkansas
and seemed to be a gutless slug
but you creeps must already
know such things.

So probe my flesh
and drink my blood,
but make me young again.

Let me dream the dream of fire.
Let me dream the dream of healing,
as if healing itself weren't a cosmic joke.

Sunflowers and Self-Pity

The blaring field of bright
yellow sunflowers
is domesticated.
Almost military,
they obediently
turn their heads
to salute the sun.
Across the highway
in a cornfield,
wild sunflowers
are taking over.

Oh, the fat-headed
domesticated ones
are seductive
(so much more fleshy
than their feral cousins)
but later this month
their heads will bow
and blacken as they await
the farmer's cold steel.
The wild ones will go
to seed and raise hell
with the crops next year.

On the southwest end
of Cowturdville, inside

a frayed nursing home,
my woman is a damned
wild sunflower.
Everyday she dances
and drops seeds on
the mud field
of my mind and
yellow flowers erupt
from my spine.

Cowardice consumes
me and I survive
by telling myself
things could be worse.
How is it a tough man
becomes so timid?
How is it a brilliant
woman's mind becomes
permanently tangled
and short-circuited?

Oh God,
if you were a man,
I'd kick your pink ass blue
and beg for forgiveness too.

A Frankenstein of the Plains

She's wearing tight Wranglers
and scuffed cowgirl boots.
When she finishes knocking back
a shot of tequila, she nods my way
and asks if the seat next to me is taken.
I shrug, do an invisible roll of the eyes,
and bite my tongue. We're the only
two customers in this redneck bar.
This woman is stridently pretty
in a Plains-weathered way.
She wants to know why
I'm drinking nonalcohol beer.
How do I tell her I don't want sex
nor do I wish to take confession.
I'm only talking to her because
I have no one to pound
my back with BenGay.

BenGay on my back.
Vicks on my chest.
Baby oil on my privates.
Clean sheets and weekly
mashed potatoes and gravy.
I desire only simple things.

But she's too simple.
She's really quite pretty

in a hard-knock rez way,
but she won't shut up, says
her boyfriend in the county
jail threatens suicide unless
she visits him every day
and the fat, red-faced bartender
is clocking her out of the corner
of his imperial blue eye and
Cowturdville does not tolerate
drunken Indians at all since it
barely tolerates sober Skins.

I need her hands, not
her mouth, but soon
my own mouth is
mincing words,
incantations of
purported innocence.
The great withered snake
of loneliness is stirring,
lost on the beige sand
between dream and waking.

No, no, no, I won't do this.
I buy her another shot
and leave my lust in a lurch.
Adiós, my girl, I got to go.

In the sanctuary of my battered Ford,
the futility of my near miss is palpable.
I decide to drive to Chadron.

There's this electric massager
I saw in Wal-Mart last week.
Its handle is shaped like
a boomerang so the user
can hit every spot on his back.
I'm going to go buy me one
and worship and writhe at
the rural church of electricity
like a Frankenstein of the Plains.

The Moon, the Moon-ee-o!

Today I bring you home from
the nursing home and char
some burgers black, but they're
still red inside so I end up giving
them to our dogs and cats.

It's dark when I drive you back.
The huge, orange moon slaps
up against the windshield
like a brand-new basketball.
You screech: *The moon, the moon.*
I rasp: *The moon, the moon-ee-o!*
We both laugh crazily.
You take your pills easily
tonight and allow the nurse
and me to dress you
for bed with no fuss.
While we're putting on
your nightgown, the nurse
brushes her breast against
my arm and smiles.
I frown as if to say:
Darling, what's the point?
Can your little tittie sweeten
my soured heart?

Later that night, alone in bed,
I reach for the moon
and shudder and glower
and thrash in the glow
of a brief liquid gloom
in a womanless room.

Good-Hearted Woman

I break you out of the nursing home, bring you to our house, and hold you on the pot until you're done. Then I clean you with a washcloth and put fresh panties on you. I lead you to the car and sit you on a thick towel, just in case.

It's a tart-lemon day in early spring. The huge drifts from El Niño are starting to melt as we cruise to Pine Ridge. On the way, we see a silly couplet occur: the sun breaks through and the skies are blue. Willie and Waylon are on the radio warbling "She's a Good-Hearted Woman" and they make us giggle. God knows why we always liked Waylon and Willie.

Almost halfway to the rez, we see a huge golden eagle rise from a rabbit carcass on the road and perch atop a telephone pole, so close we can see its eyeballs. I offer unlit Marlboros out the window. Later, when we get into Pine Ridge, I lock you in the car to prevent you from wandering. I go get the mail, a *Rapid City Journal,* and three Snickers bars.

We are happy children, driving in our warm Indian car and eating candy bars. We cruise around the disheveled town trying to find one of your brothers at home, but they are all gone, busy doing their daily rez duties.

Driving home through White Clay, we see a white teen, a clerk at Jack and Jill Market, slip on some ice outside the store and go to his knees in a mud puddle. He jumps up, brushes his pants, and upends again, this time landing on his ass. The back of his jeans are soiled with brown mud. He rises and retreats back toward the store, looking furtively over his shoulder, hoping no one has witnessed such folly.

Then, from some ethereal plane, two drunk and dire winos pop into the movie we're filming. Their dirty pants are not from mud. Oh Lord, we laugh wildly for the twenty minutes it takes to get home, all the time I'm hugging and kissing you, trying to keep from going into the ditch, thanking God for this day, and for you, my good-hearted woman. My crazy, sweet, sweet woman. My continuing life and love.

Deep into the American Ether

And so for my fiftieth birthday, I buy a new toy computer that plays CDs while I type and do searches on the Internet. It's like television, as I'm baffled and bored at the same time, but it's strangely erotic in this electronic void, so I hook up with some lonely women. For months I travel deep into the ether of their imagined flesh before I tire of the vast desert of lust. I join an Indian Lit listserv filled to the gills with white experts on Indians—a very creepy place. One white woman in the Northwest actually poses as a Blackfeet from Browning until someone who knows her points out she isn't. A Jewish woman in New York claims to own over a thousand books on Indians! No matter the subject, she knows the answer. I'm tempted to ask her if she knows how Indian cum tastes, but I don't. I simply quit the list and lose the fools.

Finally, one fine day I search for the name of an ancient lover and find it too easily. She owns a macrobiotic restaurant in a small yuppie enclave not far from the University of Wisconsin. She does have an e-mail address, and I know that the computer will allow me a certain form of time travel, but I decide not to bother her. We are better off in each other's past. Let her have her macrobiotic food. We are each entitled to our own particular brand of foolishness, but . . . Macrobiotics?

Nearing the millennium, macro-fucking-biotics . . . !
Nearing the millennium, I mark fifty years of loneliness and
draw up a list for a week's worth of canned soup and crack-
ers, dog food and dish soap, kitty litter, Marlboros, and ginko
biloba. Oh, the years of brown rice I spent with her!

Once, lost in the sixties, after I broke up with her, in the
Back Bay of Boston, wandering penniless and stoned, I
found myself badly needing a restroom. I came upon this
monstrous Gothic cathedral, brownstone grimed by city air.
I entered and could find no humans. Finally, I found a men's
room and entered a stall and sat down upon the throne. On
the wall someone had fingerpainted FUCK GOD in excre-
ment. In those days I was an on-and-off believer, and at
times as sinful as any man could be, but I was simply
shocked. What type of person could do such a thing? Well,
whoever it was, he multiplied. Screwed like a rabbit and his
progeny now inhabit the Internet.

On the news it says almost 70 percent of Internet use is sex
related. They say there are over 30,000 sex sites. I don't
know if that's true, but one day after months of searching, I
finally find a site for nude Native Americans! They aren't
Indians; they're Native Americans. Ah, the most beautiful

woman is Princess White Feathered Wind of the Cherokee Tribe. Her nipples are pert! Next best is Tasheena Shy Deer of the Apache Tribe. She has blond pubic hair . . . and she seems to have placed an earring in the wrong place. Mighty fucking amazing, these Internet Native Americans.

Red Flag

The frayed shirt, faded white
except for the bright red seams,
drapes atop the barbed wire gate
and those seams, where the dye
was heaviest, striate like arteries.

It is the blood that brings us to this place.

In the full bloom of midlife
I huff and puff to open the barbed
wire gate and drag it away as you
ride your painted pony through.
Your brown skin, burned black
by the summer sun, blinds me.

It is the blood that brings us to this place.

Your strong thighs grabbing
the pony, your tightly braided hair
and flawless teeth, the wild paradox
of your young eyes meeting mine . . .
it is all too much, too much
like some sort of final reward
before the end.

Oh, heart, pump the blood
to the parched parts that need it.
Oh, heart, don't fail us now
in this hour of need.

Indian Sign Language

Most of our communication
can be done by quirky
movements of the body.
When you're angry because of
some malfunctioning synapse,
I simply nod my head and frown
and you know I'm copiloting
your cerebral spaceship.

Today when we drove through
the flatlands to Chadron,
I turned on Public Radio and waved
my hands in the air, pretending
I was directing some orchestra.
You chortled gleefully when I passed
cars and then far beyond them
flipped them the bird like
I was some macho lowrider.

When I beeped the horn
at grazing cows, we both laughed.
Darling, I just looked at you
and twitched my head for no reason
and you laughed so freely.
I pushed my lips out and nodded
when a state trooper passed
and you giggled.

Today you were secure
with my sign language
but at the Safeway store
you screamed at some strange
fat woman for no reason.
The stunned woman's face
was crimson and her two chins
were quivering with fear.
I put my index finger
to my forehead and circled
it until the woman understood.
I'm sorry, I told her. *I'm sorry.*

Later, as we neared the folly of
Cowturdville, a goofy antelope
got on the road and stopped
directly in front of our car.
I screeched to a halt, but I could
hear its nervous, clattering
feet above the drone
of the air conditioner.

Its eyes were dark, fluttering hearts
that jumped out and kissed our eyes.
An ancient song of blood rang out
and snapped our human minds.
In an instant of lucidity, you
whispered, *Spirit, it's a spirit,*
and neither one of us laughed.

Decoration Day

You're across this shit-heeled town
in a third-rate nursing home, yet
your shimmering brain-fire
seeks and intoxicates me.
In this broiling Plains dusk,
the living membrane
of grasshoppers is
the only thing that keeps
this cheap house
of ours from crumbling
and the living membrane
of love's memory is
the only thing that keeps me
from crumbling, from curing
my illness with the Rx
of an oz. of lead . . .

For decades I've courted
the poem of lead, but I won't
write it for some years yet.
These days I write to salt
my wounds while I silently
curse the countless thousands
of castrated American poets
who use words to paint flowers
disguised as fucking flowers.

On this Decoration Day, I
wouldn't even steal *their* poetry
to brighten my unmarked grave.
Let my hole be decorated with
cheap plastic flowers, the kind
that bloom in the cemeteries
of the poor and illiterate.

Jungle Fever

According to United Nations
statistics approximately 11%
of the world population
will be reincarnated next year.
No lie, I swear it's true! I wouldn't
fib to fine citizens like you.

According to United Nations
statistics approximately 11%
of the world population
will be reincarnated next year.
Men with huge bananas will
come back with Vienna sausages.
Those stuck with Vienna sausages
will come back as women.
Women will come back as tigers,
moaning in the ecstasy
of a manless jungle.
Fetid earth, havoc of green.
Fronds of flirtation.
Flowers of fantastic intoxication.
And me in my middle-aged safari suit,
looking for a gate to get in.

Another Voice in the Wilderness

FOR HAYDEN CARRUTH

It's an electric late-March night
in the early autumn of my life.
The backyard grass is still squishy
from the slow-melting snow.

A cartoon clarity of black sky
makes the stars seem touchable.
It's a holy sky, but my human
voice is saying, *I hope I don't
step in a pile of dogshit.*

I've spent a whole lifetime
stepping into doom.
I'm an expert at that
and losing women.
These days I think of women
only in a historical context.
On many occasions in my 20s
I took comfort with several
women in a single day.
I was powerfully cursed and
could get stoned in the morning,

straighten up by noon, get drunk
at night, and wake the next
day with a clear, sweet head.

Sometimes I thank God
I survived my 20s, but then
I remind myself that I'm
at war with God at present.
And he is surely winning.
In the past four years I haven't
made history with one woman.

Three days ago I had an affair,
a quite torrid one I admit,
with my lonesome left hand.
My cats watched, astonished
enough to scowl and shake
their heads in disbelief.
I tried to tell them it was
art for art's sake.
Something like poetry.

A recent survey by the NEA
tells us 24 million people
in the U.S. write creatively
for their own fulfillment.
Of those who write, 2.3 million
reported having been published.

Can a poem have a thesis
of "spanking the monkey"

and should I report it
as having been published?
I've written several poems about
this desperate subject before.
I'm a poet. Another voice
in the wilderness. Just one of
those 2.3 million published people.

It's an electric late-March night.
The early autumn of my life.
The backyard grass is squishy
from my slow-melting life.

For the Fullblood Girl Next to Me

Cowturdville Saloon again . . .
This foolish temple of scarred
knuckles and pubic hairs.
This sad sanctuary of scared
boys lost in lust and lonely, old
women with fluttering innards.
Here in this honky-tonk
ghosts of groin bone
haunt and taunt.
I have not had a drink
in more than ten years.
So what am I doing here?
More important, why
are you here with me?
Never mind, never mind.
Just take my lonely hand.
Tell me again how wind sings
through summer cottonwoods.
Tell me again where the owls
sleep in daylight.
Tell me again how
your husband beat you
until you stabbed his
right eye out with a fork
and it ended up centered on
his plate of spaghetti.

Mon Legionaire

Magdalena . . .
Your call woke me
and I didn't know who I was.
Maybe I was you. Yes, we ran
our hand up your thigh
as you told me classes were
canceled due to the blizzard.
When you said farewell,
I returned to the desert.
Bullets violined off the sand.
The sun burnished my soul
but my kepi kept me cool.
Somewhere I could hear
Edith Piaf singing lowly
like the sweet frog she was.
The delicious morsel of a violent
death was upon my plate . . .
Then the telephone rang again.
Some stranger asking if I
would read poems at his college.
Going to be out of the country, I said
and rolled over onto my stomach
and arched into the heated dunes.
I drank a sip from my canteen
and jacked a shell into the rifle.
I took the phone off the hook

and smiled, continents away
from this acne-scarred town
of rednecks and redskins.

Jehovah Calls In Sick Again

The mad babble
from down below
is a pain in His holy ass.
Most days He shuts His windows
to the manic rain of prayers.
In the silver-clouded wilderness
of my imagined privacy, He
contemplates His options.
He *could* decide to dispatch
flame-throwing angels
to incinerate every American
male who has had the slightest
involvement with gangs.
He *could* torment them again with
a phalanx of angels disguised
as little, bug-eyed aliens.
He *could* grow hair on the breasts
of every woman who has a tattoo.
He *could* arrange for Jerry Falwell
to be caught kissing a young boy.
He *could* send blood floods, gut blizzards,
terrible tornadoes to Indian reservations
or schoolyard killers to Catholic schools,
but today He thinks . . .

He'll just doze for a while, maybe
later traipse down to the dungeon
He built for the shackled
and starving Great Spirit.

Dead Skooonk

Driving to the neurologist
in Rapid City, I cannot
draw you into dialogue.
It's been over five years
since the diminutive Chinese
MD told us your brain cells
were tangling forever.
You're silent for thirty minutes
until I take my lower dentures
and wedge them on my nose
and sing: *Dashing through the*
snow, in a one-horse open sleigh . . .

You laugh and say: *You have*
a kitten on your nose!
I repeat what you say. We
toss the phrase back and
forth for ten minutes until
we pass a dead skunk
in the middle of the road
near the Oblaya store.
You ask what it is and I
say it's a *Skooonk!*
Skooonk, I say, until you

trust the glint in my eyes.
Skooonk, you say, and
smile, content with
your mad chauffeur, your
daft cataloger of beasts.

At the Half-Century Mark,
the Desert Boy Is Dying of Thirst

The pert crocus bulging
up through the soft earth
is so laughably nasty.
The anxious sun bounces
between two too-white clouds.
Under quick-melting snow
lies shy, green grass, and
a blue jay in one of my
scraggly cedars is squawking
at a fat, red squirrel.

I'd fall to my knees if
our past walked by.
Pucker my mouth
and loving duty do.

Sweetheart, when I
brought you home today
from the piss-perfumed
nursing home, you flushed
my damn reading glasses
down the toilet and later
wedged the peanut butter
and jelly sandwich I made
you between the pages of my
new Sherman Alexie book.

I am constantly shaking my head,
not in dismay, but in wonder at
my ever-increasing love for you.
For the first time in my miserable
life, I can give unconditional love.
Five years ago, when your calamitous
disease first struck, you had
a startling moment of clarity
and told me that I should
find another woman . . .
and get on with my life.

Well, I haven't yet and I
still love you more than
you will ever comprehend,
but if I could find a woman
to come in just once a week
and hold me for five minutes
and tell me everything's going
to be okay, my life would be
so much simpler.
Yes, I know the cure for what
ails me: a kind word or two,
and, if I'm lucky, a tablespoon
of woman dew.

Star, Can You Hear Me?

Star, you must
be the North Star.
You're the brightest
blink I see tonight, but
you're little more than
a twinkling hairball
of no consequence
since I spent all my wishes
harsh lifetimes ago.
Nevertheless, my house
sure could use new rugs.
Star, can you hear me?
And I wish a plague
of herpes would hatch
on the goofy tongue
of that *mixedblood* critic
doing his wannabe dance
down to the south of me.
You know the one I mean.
Star, can you hear me?
Give it some thought and
get back to me on that.
I'll be out here driving
around this racist town
listening to Emmylou Harris
and trying to divest this

American dream of magical
something for nothing.
The fact is, Star, I'm scared
to go home to no home.
I need you to grow me
some gigantic cojones.

Cowturdville at Easter

Oh! here comes Peter Cottontail,
Hoppin' down the bunny trail,
Hippity hoppity,
Happy Easter day . . .

And I find his rear quarters
in a pool of blood on my UNWELCOME
mat on the front porch and Taco John,
sated and purring, flat on his back
in glee, is so proud of his bloody art.

I toss the legs out into the street
and my big black cat simply shrugs.
Down the block, young white trash
in pickups are drunk, practicing
the burned-rubber ballet of manhood.
Across the street on the grade school
playground, Skins are shooting hoops
and smoking dope. One kid is tossing
one-handed J's, his other hand firmly
on his waistband, the hidden pistol.
Oh! Christ, arise again this day
and do something useful.
Slam-dunk my heart through
the hoop of compassion.

Open my eyes to the lost
sight of hope or some
similar magic voodoo,
and soothe the scorpions
dancing deep in my gut.

One of the Grim Reaper's Disguises

Death does not speak
to me with meaty breath
although ancient hamburgers
dance through my veins and
the leering buffalo skull
on the wall above my couch
dribbles drool onto my heart.

At fifty, I have learned to see
the Grim Reaper in all his disguises.
I can see him in a can of Budweiser.
I can see him in a shaker of salt.
Tonight, death speaks through spuds.
On my kitchen counter a ten-pound
bag of potatoes is rabid with tendrils.
They smell like a coven of winos.
I'm afraid to go near them. They've
already strangled one of my cats.
Hey, these spuds are not vegetarians.
These are bad-ass rez potatoes.
They'll sucker-punch you
and kick you in the nuts
when you're not looking.
If they're not death
I don't know what is.

Indian Summer Gives Way
to the Land of the Rising Sun

Memory is malleable.
Memory is a scar.
Because all things return
to their source,
grace is possible.

Lakota makoce and I've been on it
nearly twenty stumbling years.
Pine Ridge is bathed in dusk.
From a bed in the IHS Hospital, I
watch clouds smoke over red earth.
They look real, like clouds in those
paintings, those oil landscapes by
that artist on PBS—that white guy
with an afro, the one who spoke
with a hillbilly drawl and used
two-inch house brushes to
daub his little masterpieces.
He died from cancer a while back,
but has been reborn in reruns.

Darkness, sneaking Marlboros
on the balcony, bugs crawling
down the back of my hospital gown.
Under the parking lot light poles,
flying insects swarm, some able
to retain luminosity and fly
so far away with it.
Fireflies? I don't know . . .
A young nurse from Fort Berthold
says there are fireflies at her home,
but none down here in the wilds
of godless South Dakota.
She puts her hand to my cheek
to check on my fever and
I shudder with loneliness.
I wish I could take her hand
and pull her silently into
the motorized bed with me.
We could share the same cigarette.
The way I feel, it might be my last.

❀

Indian macho:
If you're going to get shot,

you might as well have a Marlboro
dangling from your lips . . . enit?
On the road below the hospital,
a young woman is running from
her drunk boyfriend. He pants,
swears, and sweats up the hill
after her, but she is too fast,
too sober.

Days drag through the unseasonable
warmth of late fall that white
people call Indian summer.
It's Indian summer
all year long around here
and through my medicinal haze
I think I hear the nurse say she'll
cook me a steak when I heal.

Memory is malleable.
Memory is a scar.
Because all things return
to their source,
grace is possible.
The simple vision of a brown
woman cooking over a stove
is a good reason to live.
But I get no steak. Instead, she
thrusts a tube up my nose and
then down into my stomach.

Ghastly brown liquid bubbles
into a glass cauldron.
I thrash and moan and wonder
who those green men are who
sit at the foot of my bed.

I am entering a faraway land.
The Indian Health Service ambulance
bumps along the dirt road, exhaust
fumes filling this tin can where I lie
like a fat sardine upon the bed, stench
from the exhaust choking, my stomach
in flames, I'm feverish, the smoking
ambulance rips down the road and up
toward Rapid City like it was in
a Road Runner cartoon.

Then, I'm in Regional Hospital.
The surgeon says the X-rays look
like colon cancer. She smiles.
I smile back and wink and
resign myself to my clichéd fate.
I am entering a faraway land.
For all I know, it could be Japan.

There are weeks that I know nothing
about when my kidneys shut down,

when my lungs shut down, when
I nearly pass on to the spirit world.
There's no bright light, I do not float
above my bed, but Colleen, you keep
coming back to me, your sweet softness,
the innocent mist you're in now,
this reservation where I found you,
where I look for you, where I cannot
find you, the past, the present, all mixed,
mixed in this faraway land, and you're
so soft, wearing a long blue skirt, so soft
and so lost and your family is taking
care of you since I cannot now . . .
but as usual, they're not doing
a good job and they lose you.

Somehow the idea comes to write
a book with paintings, watercolors
of Mexican peasant plates, each plate
will tell a story. It's bizarre, but I see
myself forward, out of the hospital
and healing. I'll set up an easel in my
backyard and paint the pictures, each
painting a chapter in my life, each
earthenware plate bordered by bright
flowers and dancing calaveras.

Even in my sickness, I know it's a
crazy idea, but then for a month I waver

between madness and extreme madness.
I believe I have cancer though the doctors
tell me daily that I don't. The thing that
sustains me, keeps me going, is apple juice.
Apple juice grows in the basement of
the hospital where old Jewish women
squeeze the sweet wetness from gray mud.
They dribble it into vials—I drink it and
my life continues. And in this basement
people float like balloons near the ceiling
and one of these people is a little monkey
dressed in a black suit and top hat.
He wears a beard and glasses.
This monkey talks to me.
I don't know why, but I believe
it is a Japanese monkey. Maybe it's
because he screams: PEARL HARBOR!
Frightened by the screeching simian,
I scream back: *ENOLA GAY!*
And my mad Mexican plates fly
around the room and smash
into smithereens.

Every imaginable type of ghost
is dancing in my room.
I'm sick and stoned beyond stone.
Toxic encephalopathy.
My brain, my entire body is poisoned.
I am a toxic half-breed!

A loony and languid viper
hissing on the doorsteps of hell.
What have I done to deserve this?

Hank Williams is under my bed
singing "Ramblin' Man" and I've
got plastic tubes up my penis
and down my throat, in my wrist
and chest and stomach. A huge
stitched trench runs from my
solar plexus to my belly button.
My American river of madness
pisses against all reason, flowing west
from Reno to San Francisco and then
east to Rapid City to St. Paul and then
into Cambridge, Mass. All these
cities merge into brick sameness.
All these cities are America and all
the red bricks are dried Indian blood.
In this city called "America" there
is a small tavern in the fog
named the *Ribeltad Vorden* or maybe
the *Plough and Stars* and it's filled
with derelicts, Indians, and artists.
I buy a pint of good Irish whiskey
and drop it in the pocket of my raincoat
where it clinks up against a chrome .45
and my brother-in-law Duane is there
in an ill-fitting, itchy tweed suit.
Duane's a tribal detective so I ask
if the Japanese doctors who implanted

the golden wire from the base of my brain
to my coccyx have cured the cancer
and he says Yeah, hell yeah.
I give him the chrome automatic and tell
him I plan to give one to all his brothers.
And how is sweet-crazy Colleen I ask.
Waiting, he says. *She's waiting for you.*

The flights to Japan were killers.
And the Japanese not only cured me,
but they harvested a kidney
without my permission.
*Like it was me who raised
the flag on Iwo Jima . . .*

The jets were long and lean lungfish.
Like some mad, mutant mixture
of Ahab and Jonah, I was
the only rider on most trips.
The aisles were windswept
and cellophane overhead ran
the length of the plane.
A howling wind whooshed the plastic
making me cry each time we landed.

On one flight, an ancient lover, now gray
and beaten, sat behind me and drooled.
She said they stole her kidney too.
Said she was a bag lady now!

That it was all my fault.
That if only I had stayed within
the realm of her sweet and mothering
love such disasters would never
have befallen us and all I can do
is nod, stare into her eyes, and cry.

Strange, how it took me a month
to believe I didn't have cancer,
and had never been to Japan.
They did remove a huge chunk
of my colon and gave me a colostomy
bag that I'd have to wear for six fragrant
months, but I never had cancer,
I never had the fucking Big C . . .
I didn't, did I?

Now, it's a year later and
somewhere in this airless
examining room I can almost
hear my young redheaded surgeon
and her young surgeon husband
doing the dirty deed atop
this Danish-modern furniture.

It's now been one year since surgery.
My vibrant MD enters, all smiles, and
says, "You're lookin' good!" But there

are many other things she tells me
as she looks at my chart, things I do not
recall at all, like how I stood atop my
bed and screamed I was a poet.
How I ripped loose my colostomy
bag and beaned a nurse with it.
How they tied me down for weeks,
stuck a tube down my soul,
and fed me life.

I'm embarrassed, but I am alive.
I thank the spirits for deleting
those memories. Memory *is*
malleable. Memory *is* a scar.
Because all things return
to their source, grace *is* possible.
One of these days I just might fly
to the Land of the Rising Sun
and thank those doctors.
Domo arigato!
Sushi?
Banzai!
Remember Pearl Harbor?

Adiós Again, My Blessed Angel
of Thunderheads and Urine

Ah, so there you are, somewhere between
the Demerol and the morphine, silently emptying
my catheter jug. Don't do that, I want to say,
but my voice is lost from two weeks on the
ventilator. Baby Girl, I want to say hello,
say I know your name, say how much I've
always loved you, but only a rasp comes
and then you are gone forever again.

I know I've got a crinkled picture of you
boxed somewhere in my shuttered house.
The image is as foreign as it is faded.
Somewhere west of Tulsa, you are leaning
against a black VW Bug, smiling and pointing
at a remarkable formation of thunderheads
that tower and bluster miles past heaven.
Your long black hair dances below your waist.
Your worn navy bell-bottoms are snug against
your perfect legs, your strong, loving hips.
And after I snap the photo, you tell me
you're going back to nursing school.
Me, I'll wander in the wilderness for thirty years
before I see you again, and then it will be only for
a minute while you empty my urine bucket
and I try to cough up words that will not
come like the flashing pain beneath
my sutures that signals healing and wonder.

Old Friend in the Dark

I've never been in a bad car crash,
but I've been on this same hospital
floor for a month and a half so I
know you can and can't hear me.
You are a shadow in a shadow land.
Yes, I've been to the country you're in.
Huge black birds float by and whisper.
When you squeak out fear, they shrug
and coo softness. Do not fear them.
Do not fear the green-faced men
who sit on the edge of your bed.
They are only green with envy.
Stand with me, let's look at you.
What glassy eyes, your brown skin is
stretched over the pale heart of fear.
Let's sing of hot Dakota summer nights.
Let's sing of frybread smell and ice-cold
beer, the sexy eyes of sweet, dark women,
and the dust of cars and kids and ghosts.
Let's sing of everyone, young and strong.
Let's dance backward
to the strength of summer.
Wake up now, friend,
and come back home.

Announcing a Change in the Menu at Neah Bay, Washington

The Makah Indians
want to resuscitate their
ancient roots, so they decide
to assassinate a gray whale.
They hand-hew a canoe
out of cedar according
to primeval specifications.
News cameras capture
a high-speed boat towing
this canoe near a whale.
The mighty Makah warriors
harpoon the thrashing hulk
and then still the waters
by blasting it in the head
with a .50-caliber rifle.
A .50-caliber rifle can kill a tank!
Another goofy chapter in
the history of American Indians.
And for the Makah, there will be
no dreams of distant McDonald's.
For the next six months, maybe a
year, it's whale burgers for breakfast
and blubber pie for dessert. And
nightmares about the crazy whites
who march in a Seattle candlelight
vigil a few days after the hunt,
carrying signs that say:
SAVE THE WHALES, KILL A MAKAH.

Verdell Redux

From a pungent blob
of ectoplasm and prairie dust,
my old Budweiser buddy materializes.
It's five years since I've seen Verdell.
He's on crutches, standing in
the doorway of the pawn shop.
He's been sober for four, but now
is missing a foot to diabetes.
Gonna be a good man
until I die. He smiles.
Gonna get into heaven,
give Jesus a big hug,
and drive my shank
into his kidneys.

Jesus! I say.
You got that right, he answers
and reaches into his grimy coat
and miraculously retrieves
a cordless shaver. Begins
running it over his face
right there on the street.
At one time that wouldn't
have bothered me.
I really must be getting old.
I tell him I got to go and
slowly edge away from him.

Death is a kitten, he says.
A warm, cuddly kitten.

I turn and nod, and mew adieu.

For My Occasional Kitten

There's one kind favor I'll ask of you
See that my grave is kept clean.
—Blind Lemon Jefferson

The claw marks on my back
are fresh and clotted with blood.
Good things come to those who wait?
I wish I could honestly describe
how your youthful purring
soothes my profane soul.
I am a scar on two legs.
I don't believe in angels,
so you must be a spirit,
but damnit, I am not dead.
Brilliant, loving pain
dances on my back
and front, ah my front!
How many centuries
have I waited for
the calamitous silence
at the end of love?

Turquoise Blues

Colleen, I stand your ground
and I'm trying like hell to stand
my ground, but the mad earth
always dances away from my feet.
Maybe that's why I've decided
to learn to run again.

This black New Mexico interstate
with the starless blue night over
it is the same one we traveled.
You'd like the sweet showroom
smell of this brand-new Buick and
country radio blaring incongruously:
You're the reason
God made Oklahoma . . .

Do not be alarmed by
the falsehoods I've created.
That tall brown girl half my age
asleep with her head on my lap
is really only make-believe.
This is a poem, after all. You know
I'd never abandon you. I made
that promise and I'll keep it
if it's the last damn thing I do.

I have been exhausted for some
years now and the tired angels

of my imagination line up
like Nevada cathouse whores:
tired, slightly disheveled,
but they're freshly douched.
Heavy perfume blankets the stink
of their scars, and when they raise
rumpled wings to sing *hallelujah,*
I see small devils scurry from
their hairy armpits.

This poem is one
of those selfish little imps.
That tall brown girl half my age
asleep with her head on my lap?
She's only make-believe, and even
if she weren't, I know you'd
cut me some slack.
I know you'd understand.

Colleen, can you see that dead coyote
in the middle of the road?
Tonight, the love we had
is that coyote, lifeless, but still
fanged and demanding attention.
Let me indulge in this brief
recreation without all this guilt.

Red dawn will soon be rising
and I have every reason
to believe that you would
understand this folly
if you only could.

The Promise

Darling, we wore
the brilliant crown
of love, although
occasional garnets
of anger throbbed
like migraines.

Our half-breed
hearts were hard,
scabrous, and so
utterly umber.
A broken world
disgorged us,
trembling upon
her fractious skin.
We arrived as
damaged goods,
abandoned at birth
and again at death.

Years ago you
would have laughed
so hard if I told you
how Verdell said
death is a cuddly kitten!
If death is a kitten,
then I'm a rabid mutt
who'll rip its head off.

Colleen, my endless
mourning could be
stopped abruptly if
I accepted the fact
that you are dead.
But if you're dead,
then I'm bringing
Pepsi and Marlboros
to a ghost.

Listen,
when the chokecherries
ripen, you'll hear me call.
When the grasshoppers
wither, I'll be standing
with you.

Upon the ghost road,
hand in hand,
our dry lips dark
with cherry blood,
we'll sing our song
of what was us.
When the chokecherries
ripen, look for me.

I'll be there, I promise.

Dancing up a dust storm
with all our lost days.

About the Author

A half-breed Indian, Adrian C. Louis was born and raised in Nevada and is an enrolled member of the Lovelock Paiute Tribe. From 1984 to 1998, he taught at Oglala Lakota College on the Pine Ridge Reservation of South Dakota. Prior to this, Louis edited four Native newspapers, including a stint as managing editor of *Indian Country Today*.

Louis has written eight books of poems, including *Fire Water World*, winner of the 1989 Poetry Center Book Award from San Francisco State University, and he is the author of two works of fiction: *Skins*, a novel, and a collection of short stories, *Wild Indians & Other Creatures*.

Louis has won various writing awards, among them a Pushcart Prize and fellowships from the Bush Foundation, the National Endowment for the Arts, and the Lila Wallace–Reader's Digest Fund. In 1999, he was elected to the Nevada Writers Hall of Fame. He currently resides in Minnesota and teaches at Southwest State University.